Introduction

The story in this book is about a Celtic farming family who lived about the time of the second Roman invasion of Britain in AD 43. The Celtic culture had been flourishing in Britain for many years before then, ever since the first Celtic tribes had arrived from Central Europe in about 800 BC.

The Celts lived mostly in scattered family farms. They were excellent farmers and metalworkers. They introduced the use of iron into northern Europe. They also invented many iron farming implements which were used for centuries after their way of life had disappeared.

Celtic farmers grew wheat, oats and barley. Cattle were kept to plough and to provide meat, milk and hides. Small, skinny sheep provided wool and milk. The Celts also kept goats, pigs and chickens.

The Celts were brave and enthusiastic warriors. They fought many battles against other tribes but also quarrelled furiously among themselves. They were no match for the organized might of the Roman army, which finally defeated them, after many years of fighting, in the first century AD.

Historians and archaeologists have found out about the life of the Celts from several different sources. Roman travellers in Europe wrote about the Celtic peoples that they met on their journeys. They discussed the Celts' appearance, their love of wine and of fighting, and told us a little about their beliefs. Some of the beautiful metal objects made by the Celts have survived and have been discovered accidentally. Archaeologists have excavated many hill-top sites where the Celts are known to have lived, and have found out about their buildings, their food, and the animals they kept from the remains discovered there.

This book tells the story of a year in the life of a Celtic child and his family. At the end of the book, you can see some detailed pictures of the tools and equipment that they might have used in their daily life. There are also suggestions for places to visit and books to read.

An Accident in the Woods

It was a bright morning in early spring. Anted stamped on the frosty ground, trying to warm his chilly feet.

'Hurry up!' Cuno, his father, called to him from the gateway. Anted tugged at the harness of the slow-moving oxen, to make them walk faster.

They were on their way to the new field near the woods. Anted felt proud to be leading the plough team. Last year, the men had said he was too young for such an important task. He had to be content with odd jobs to do around the farm.

The field they were going to plough had been cleared from the forest last year. Anted remembered how hard they had all worked. They had felled the trees with axes, dragged out the useful timber and burnt all the undergrowth. Then Cuno had yoked the ox-team to the great plough and, with much cursing and groaning, has struggled to push the heavy ploughshare through the unbroken soil.

A CELTIC FARMER

Macdonald

Contents

Introduction   5

An Accident in the Woods   6

The Roman Soldier   8

Beltane Festival   10

Haymaking   12

Harvesting   14

A Visit to the Town   16

Vorta the Blacksmith   18

New Horseshoes   20

Repairing the Thatch   22

The Boar Hunt   24

The Romans Return   26

Picture Glossary   28

Finding Out More   30

This year, they planned to grow wheat in the new field. Cuno hoped to sell his wheat to the Romans, who had established a camp not far away. The Romans had come to Britain with their army last summer. They had been trading with the people in Anted's district for many years, so there had been no fighting. But there were still sometimes soldiers to be seen near the farm, marching off on campaign.

'More customers for our grain,' Cuno had said.

Anted and his father reached the new field.

'Now, let's get this plough working!' Together, they checked the oxen's harness. Anted took his place by the leading animal, eager to guide its steps. His father grasped the plough and the ox-team lumbered into action.

'Why have you stopped, boy? Keep those oxen moving!' Cuno sounded angry. Perhaps Anted was too young to help, after all, he thought. But then he looked to where his son was pointing. There was something moving at the edge of the woods. It was a Roman cavalry horse. Nearby was the motionless figure of a Roman soldier.

The Roman Soldier

Anted had run back to the farmstead to get help. His uncles had left their work there and had helped Cuno carry the injured Roman soldier down the hillside to the farmhouse.

Now the Roman lay unconscious on a blanket near the fire. Anted looked at him curiously. Unlike his tall father and uncles, with their manes of fair hair and drooping moustaches, this man was short and stocky, with dark hair cropped close to his head. His clean-shaven face was streaked with blood. His clothes, too, were unlike the Celtic tunics and trousers that the men of Anted's family wore.

'Don't disturb him, child, he's very ill!' Anted's grandmother came up beside him, carrying a bowl filled with a steaming mixture. 'See,' she said to Anted, 'I'll bathe his wounds, and, if the gods are willing, these herbs will help him to recover.'

Their voices disturbed the Roman. He stirred in his sleep and mumbled some words which Anted could not understand. The Roman opened his eyes. He frowned, and looked slowly round the room. He tried to get up, but fell back with a sudden cry of pain.

'It's his leg,' explained Anted's grandmother. 'It's broken. He won't be able to walk properly for weeks. It must have happened when he fell from his horse.'

She knelt down beside the Roman and gently patted his hand. 'We are friends,' she said, smiling. The Roman frowned again, and then smiled back.

'I understand,' he said, in their own Celtic language, 'I also friend.' Then he groaned, and turned his head away. His eyes closed, and he slipped back into unconsciousness.

Anted's father came across the room.

'Mother,' he said, 'we shall have to straighten that leg of his and put it in a splint. Anted, go out to the woodpile and fetch two long, sturdy pieces of wood, the best you can find.' 'And you two,' he said, turning to Anted's uncles, 'we'll need you to hold the poor man while we deal with his leg. It's a painful business.'

Anted's father and grandmother worked quickly to straighten the broken bone and to bind the wooden splint securely to the Roman's leg with strips of linen cloth.

'That will keep his leg still while the ends of the broken bone join together again,' Anted's grandmother told him. She made a special medicine for the Roman to drink to take away his pain. He did not wake up again for three whole days and nights.

9

Beltane Festival

It was now several days since Anted and Cuno had found the Roman soldier. He was still very weak, but grandmother's medicines were working, and he was slowly beginning to recover. He had told them that his name was Petronius, and that he was an officer in the Roman Army's Second Legion. He had learned to speak some of Anted and Cuno's Celtic language on earlier visits to Britain, when he had traded with Celtic farmers who wanted to sell their grain to the Roman soldiers.

Now he sat propped up outside the farmhouse in the spring sunshine, watching Anted and his family preparing for the great festival of Beltane.

'Tell me,' he said to Anted, who was sitting beside him, 'why are they building those huge bonfires? And what is that strange figure made of twigs and straw?'

Anted explained. 'Every year, we have a great feast with the other farmers around here to give thanks to the gods for bringing us safely through the winter.'

Anted's mother came out of the farmhouse to scatter grain for her chickens to eat, and joined in their conversation. 'This year, our farmstead has been chosen to hold the feast. So we are building bonfires and a straw man to burn. Soon you will see our neighbours arriving with their cattle. When the fires are lit, they will lead the animals through the smoke to drive away evil spirits. The straw man is an offering to the goddess. If she is pleased, she will give us a good harvest this year.'

As they were talking, a tall, stern figure in long robes strode across the farmyard to where Anted and Petronius were sitting. 'That's Falco, the druid,' whispered Anted. 'He's come to lead the prayers at the festival.'

Later, while the bonfires glowed and the straw man blazed, Anted and Petronius watched as Falco raised his arms and chanted over and over again, 'All is well! Goddess, accept our offerings. Bless our crops! May the year be fruitful!'

11

Haymaking

Anted was hot and thirsty. The dust from the field swirled around him, irritating his throat. He leaned on the hoe he was using to chop down all the weed seedlings, and sighed. He was standing in the new field by the woods, where he had first caught sight of the injured Petronius. It seemed a long time ago.

Now, wheat grew tall and green in the field. The druid's prayers had been answered and it looked like being a good crop. 'The trouble is,' said Anted to himself, 'there's a bumper crop of weeds, too!'

A sudden rasping noise made Anted look up. It came from two fields away. Shielding his eyes against the strong summer sunlight, Anted could see a group of figures standing on the edge of the hay meadow. The noise he had heard was the sound of sickles being sharpened against whetstones. Glad of an excuse to stop his weeding, Anted dropped his hoe and ran across to join the others. Haymaking had begun!

'Hello there, my friend!' Petronius greeted Anted as he arrived, rather out of breath, in the meadow. 'Come to help us, then?' Petronius was much better now. He could walk quite well with the help of the crutch which one of Anted's uncles had made for him. To everyone's surprise, he had proved to be quite knowledgeable about farming.

'I am a soldier,' he had told them, 'but my family has a farm outside Rome. We grow different crops there – olives and grapes as well as wheat – but let me help you as much as I can while I am your guest.'

The whole family, with Petronius helping, was soon hard at work in the hay meadow, cutting the sweet-smelling grass with the newly-sharpened sickles and heaping it into long rows to dry. It was back-breaking work.

'Pray to the gods for fine weather, son,' Cuno had said. 'We need the sunshine to dry the grass to make hay. Then we will have food for our animals during the winter.'

Harvesting

'Will you really leave us soon, Petronius?' Anted asked. He had grown fond of the Roman and was sad to think that he might be going.

They were standing on the harvest field, looking at the ripe wheat. This year was quite the best harvest Anted had ever seen.

Petronius nodded. 'I'm so much better now, thanks to your family,' he said. 'I have to think of joining the Legion again soon. It is my duty. Your father was telling me that he had received news from a travelling merchant. My fellow-soldiers will soon be coming back to the army camp nearby. You remember I told you that they were planning to march westwards in the spring? Now I want to hear how they got on and whether the tribes they met were friendly or hostile. Perhaps, too, the officers will have news from my own country. I would love to know how my family are. I have a brother not much older than you, you know.'

Anted frowned. 'I will miss you when you go,' he said. 'You must promise to come back to see us again.'

'Of course,' said Petronius. 'Now, back to work, or your father will be angry. There's such a lot to do.'

They bent down again to pluck the ripe heads of wheat from the stalks, and to heap them into large baskets. Anted's and Petronius' arms were almost raw from the scratching of the prickly stalks and their eyes were red and sore from the dust and the flying seeds. But Anted knew that without wheat there would be no bread or porridge to eat, and nothing to sell or exchange for other goods they needed.

Back at the farm, Anted's uncles spread the ears of wheat on the ground and beat them with heavy sticks to loosen the grains from the husks. Anted's mother and grandmother tossed the grains up in the air, using special shallow baskets, to let the inedible husks fly away in the breeze. Anted helped them to gather the loose grain into sacks, ready to store for the winter. Petronius helped with the oxen, who were kept busy all day carting grain to the granaries. They deserved a special feed after all their hard work. The harvest would soon be safely over for another year.

A Visit to the Town

Anted, Cuno and Petronius were standing in the busy market place of the nearby town. Anted looked around with interest. There was such a lot to see, and noise and bustle everywhere. You could buy or barter anything – food, fine leather, linen cloth, jewellery.

Cuno had come to town to buy another pair of oxen to pull the plough. Anted and Petronius were going to visit the workshop belonging to Vorta the blacksmith.

16

He had promised to fit iron horseshoes on to Petronius' horse, in preparation for the Roman's journey back to his Legion.

A small crowd of people was gathering in one corner of the market place. Anted could hear them shouting and cheering. 'What's going on?' he asked. 'Follow me,' said Cuno. 'We'll soon find out.'

Everyone was watching two huge, powerful men. They were wrestling, each trying to throw the other to the ground according to the Celts' rules for the sport.

'That's my cousin, Rosco!' said Cuno, excitedly. 'The one with the red hair. Just look at that!' he exclaimed, as the two men swayed and grunted. 'He nearly had him on the floor, that time! Good man, Rosco. Keep at it!'

As he was talking, a great roar went up from the crowd. Some cheered, the rest groaned. Rosco had managed to catch the other wrestler off guard, and, with a great heave of his shoulders, had flipped the man into the air. His opponent fell with a heavy thud, flat on his back. Rosco had won!

All around them, people were arguing. A scuffle broke out close to Anted and Petronius. Cuno shepherded them both away from the wrestlers.

'It's time we left,' he said. 'Too much drink and too many hot tempers. I'm going to look at cattle. You two go and find Vorta.'

17

Vorta the Blacksmith

The blacksmith's forge was shrouded in smoke. As Anted and Petronius drew near, they could hear the clang of hammer blows on iron. They were welcomed at the doorway by a shower of sparks. Vorta the smith looked up at them. His shock of ginger hair and great straggling moustache made him look like a wild man.

'Welcome, Anted,' he bellowed. 'Where's your father? And who's this you've brought with you?' Anted explained that Cuno had sent him to ask Vorta to shoe the Roman's horse. Anted had to shout, too, since Vorta had grown deaf after years of working at his noisy trade.

'A Roman horse, eh! We should be able to do that tomorrow. Now, stay and watch this, if you like. We're going to put this iron tyre on that cartwheel over there.'

18

Vorta called to his assistant. Together they heaved the iron tyre into the red-hot bed of charcoal in the fire. The bellows pumped and, slowly, the iron band began to glow, dull red at first and then brighter and brighter until it shone like the sun. Then Vorta and his assistant took a pair of tongs each and gripped the glowing tyre. In one practised movement, they lifted the tyre, centred it over the wheel and dropped it into place.

'Now the water!' roared Vorta. His assistants rushed to fling water over the wheel from the wooden buckets which stood ready. A cloud of steam and a smell of scorching wood filled the air. 'More water, more water!' called Vorta, impatiently. The air gradually cleared.

'It's a good fit,' said Vorta, picking up the wheel as if it had been no heavier than a sparrow's feather. He ran his hand around the iron tyre.

The metal had shrunk as it cooled and now gripped the wooden wheel tightly. Vorta reached for his hammer and with a few hefty blows, made the final adjustments to the fit. He turned to face them.

'Tomorrow then,' he smiled. 'Your horse. Before sunset. I'll be waiting for you!'

19

New Horseshoes

Anted and Petronius had stayed overnight in the
town. Rosco, the wrestler, and his wife had made them
very welcome. At supper, Petronius had amazed the
Celts with his stories of fights between gladiators in
the Arena at Rome. There, men from all corners of
the Roman world fought with spears, nets and knives,
while the vast crowd cheered their favourites and
hissed the losers.

Now, Anted and Petronius were leading Petronius'
horse to the blacksmith's forge. They walked past
rows of tall wooden storehouses. Anted explained that
grain was kept there, to feed the townspeople during
the winter and to provide seed for next year's crops.

'We have huge storehouses for grain, too,'
Petronius said. 'We have to keep a supply to feed the
thousands of people who live in the big city of Rome.
But over there, we have tame cats to guard the grain.
They kill the rats and mice who come to steal it.'

20

They arrived at Vorta's forge. Vorta nodded cheerfully to Anted and Petronius and went over to the horse. He stroked its muzzle and talked to it in a low, comforting voice. Vorta lifted each of its hooves in turn, to see what size shoes it would need. Turning to a basket of horseshoes, he picked out four, and put them into the furnace to get hot.

'Here, boy, you hold the horse's head while I'm shoeing him,' boomed Vorta. He worked swiftly, nailing the hot shoes onto each hoof in turn. Petronius was fascinated. He had never seen a horse shod before.

'There,' laughed Vorta, 'all done! That will make the journey easier for him. You'll need to come back for a new set next spring, though!'

Petronius thanked him, and offered to pay for the horseshoes, but Vorta refused to accept his money.

'Take it as a gift from the Celts,' he said.

Repairing the Thatch

'Go and put your tunic on! You'll catch your death of cold!' High on the farmhouse roof, Anted shivered. His mother was right. Summer was over, and every day there was more mist and rain. The first of the autumn gales had ripped a hole in the thatched roof of the farmhouse. Anted and Cuno were working hard to repair the damage before more storms came. Cuno had climbed to the top of the ladder, and was arranging fresh bundles of straw to cover the hole in the roof. He hammered in v-shaped wooden pegs to hold the straw in place.

From his seat high on the roof, Anted could see other members of his family working busily at various tasks around the farmyard.

His mother and sister chatted together as they plastered daub onto the woven walls of the new byre. When it was finished, it would keep their cattle warm and dry during the winter. Anted could see two of his cousins busily mixing more daub for the walls. They stirred the sticky mixture of clay and animal hair in the daub pit, using wooden paddles. Anted could hear them laughing at the strange slurping noises it made.

'Hello, Uncle, look at me!' Anted waved to his uncle, who was working on the roof of the new byre. His uncle waved back, and then returned to his task, frowning with concentration. He would need to work very fast to get the thatch finished before the winter frosts set in.

Beyond the new byre, Anted could see his grandmother washing clothes in a wooden tub. He called to her, too, but she didn't hear him.

'I wonder what Petronius is doing now?' Anted said to himself. 'Is he marching to battle with his Legion, or has he left Britain to visit his own country? I hope he comes back to see us soon.'

'Wake up, daydreamer!' Cuno's loud voice made Anted jump. 'Hey, hold on tight! We don't want you to break your leg as well! Climb down that ladder and bring some more pegs up here for me, please. We're nearly finished.'

23

The Boar Hunt

It was very early in the morning. A chilly mist hung round the farmstead, but Anted hardly noticed the cold. He was going on his first boar hunt today! He held his new hunting knife proudly. Anted's fingers traced the swirling decorations carved on its handle, and ran gently along its sharp blade. He thought that it was the best knife in the world.

'Right, men, we're off!' Cuno and the other hunters whistled to their dogs, picked up their spears and strode out of the farmyard. Anted hurried after them, anxious not to be left behind. They all set off towards the still-dark forest. Once among the trees, they moved stealthily along the tracks made by deer and wild boar through the undergrowth. The dogs ran backwards and forwards, busily sniffing at all kinds of enticing scents. Startled wild birds cawed and flapped overhead. Anted's legs were scratched and stung by brambles and nettles, but, in his excitement, he ignored the pain.

Suddenly, Cuno's best dog stood very still, sniffing the air. Cuno signalled to the hunters to stop moving and listen. The forest was strangely still and silent. Anted was frightened. He was glad he was not alone among the tall trees.

All at once, the silence was shattered as the dogs began to bark and bay, hurling themselves forward through the bushes. Anted gasped. Now he could see five or six wild boar in a clearing only a little way ahead. For a split second, the boar were too frightened to move. There was just time for Cuno to hurl his spear towards the nearest animal. The other men rushed forward, following the dogs, with their spears at the ready. They killed three boars altogether. The rest escaped.

Later, Cuno showed Anted how to gut and clean the dead boar with his new hunting knife. They carried their quarry home, slung upside down between poles. Tomorrow there would be a great feast at the farm, with plenty of roast boar to eat.

The Romans Return

All morning, Cuno and Anted had been preparing the boar for the spit. Anted had used his new knife to shave off the prickly bristles from the boar's skin as his father had shown him. Then they had tied the boar to the spit and set it over an open fire to roast slowly.

Now it was evening, and Cuno and his family were gathered around the table set up in the courtyard under the bright stars. A great flickering fire had been lit to keep everyone warm. Anted noticed that there was a place empty at the table. He was about to mention it when he heard the sound of horses' hooves. Suddenly, Petronius was there, looking splendid in his armour and cloak. Leaping down from his horse, he saluted Cuno and Anted's mother and swept Anted into a great bear hug. Another Roman soldier stood beside him, smiling broadly.

'Now the feast can really begin!' cried Cuno. 'Sit down, Petronius, and take some wine and bread. We are going to eat the boar that Anted and I killed yesterday. And ask your friend to sit down as well.'

'With pleasure,' smiled Petronius, 'but first I have gifts for the family that looked after me so well.' Petronius had brought fine purple cloth for Anted's grandmother and an enormous amphora of wine for Cuno. For Anted's mother he had brought two little striped furry animals with large green eyes. 'These are cats from the land of Egypt,' he told her. 'They are small now, but will grow quickly and keep your grain store free from mice and rats.' Then he smiled down at Anted.

'And to you, my dear friend and companion of the summer, I give the finest battle sword of the Roman Army.' And he unbuckled his own sword and laid it in Anted's arms.

Anted was speechless with joy for a moment. Then he stumbled to his feet and reached for the hunting knife at his belt.

'Petronius, in return I give you this British dagger. A gift for a gift, an honour returned.' He sat down amid clapping and cheering. Cuno nodded to his son. Anted had done the right thing. Then the feasting began.

Picture Glossary

Horses and their equipment

The Celts were excellent horsemen and invented the iron horseshoe. Bronze ceremonial horse gear has also been found: the drawings here show a terret (the ring through which the driving reins of a chariot pass), a bit and a metal joining piece for leather straps.

A decorated wagon

Bronze decorated wagon, probably ceremonial, found in Denmark. Wagons like this had roller bearings of wooden pins in a bronze case, which made it easier for the wheel to turn on the axle.

Farming tools

A selection of Celtic tools: bill-hook for pruning (1), sickle (2), chisel (3), file (4), iron chisel (5), axe (6), adze (7), saw (8), hammer (9), knife (10), and tongs (11).

The *vallus* or reaping machine, shown at the bottom of the opposite page, was invented about 100 years after the story in this book. The machine is pushed by a mule or ox, and guided by a man. A large comb-like blade cuts ears of corn and sweeps them into a box.

terret

joining piece

bit

horseshoe

The Celts
The Celts originally came from Central Europe. This map shows how they spread out all over Europe between 800 BC and the first century AD.

Pottery
A selection of British Celtic pottery used before the Romans came.

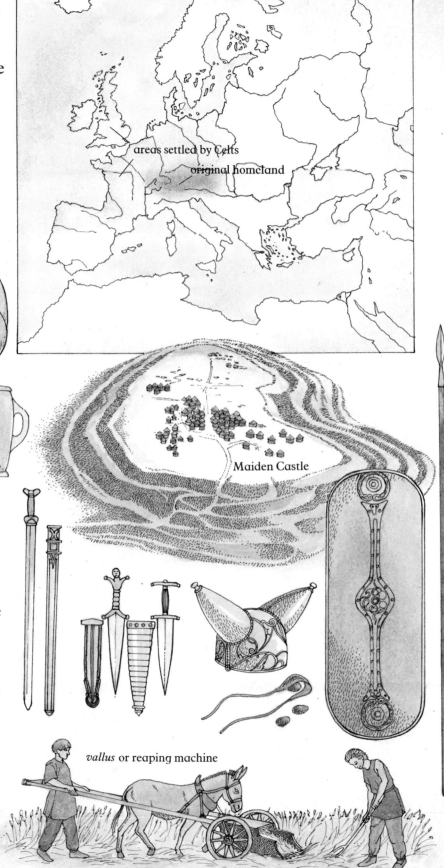

areas settled by Celts

original homeland

Maiden Castle

Weapons and Forts
The Celts were brave and inventive warriors. They used swords and iron-tipped spears. The bronze daggers, helmet and shield shown here were probably for ceremony only, but similar weapons and armour would have been used in battle. Maiden Castle in Dorset was a Celtic fort which could shelter up to 5,000 people. In spite of its earthwork defences it fell to the Romans in AD 43.

vallus or reaping machine

Finding Out More

Books to Read

The following books contain information about the Celts and their way of life, and also about Roman soldiers of the same period:

P. J. Reynolds **Farming in the Iron Age** Cambridge University Press 1977

P. J. Reynolds **Cassivellanus, the Celtic King** (booklets in the History First series) Cambridge University Press 1978

R. Place **The Celts** Macdonald Educational 1977

E. Abranson **Roman Legionaries at the time of Julius Caesar** Macdonald Educational 1979

P. Connolly **The Roman Army** Macdonald Educational 1975

G. Caselli **The Roman Empire and the Dark Ages** Macdonald Educational 1981

You will need an adult to help you to read the following books, but they contain a lot of fascinating information:

T. G. E. Powell **The Celts** Thames and Hudson 1974

A. Ross **Everyday Life of the Pagan Celts** Batsford 1970